The Equestrian's

Journey To

Self-Confidence

By Patricia Reszetylo

The information in this book is meant to supplement, not replace, proper equestrian training. Like any sport involving speed, equipment, balance and environmental factors, equestrianism poses some inherent risk. The authors and publisher advise readers to take full responsibility for their safety and know their limits. Before practicing the skills described in this book, be sure that your equipment is well maintained, and do not take risks beyond your level of experience, aptitude, training, and comfort level.

ISBN-13: 978-1519678119

ISBN-10: 1519678118

Table of Contents

Welcome!

Hi! I'm Patricia Reszetylo, an equestrian and horse lover much like yourself. I've been in love with these magnificent beasts since I was 9 years old, and an owner since I was 12.

As an adult, I sustained some (non-horse-related) injuries, and realized I didn't bounce as well as I used to – but worked through that fear, riding my horse in the back pasture in a 30-meter circle for several months.

Then I took a gainer off him – at a panicked gallop, no less, and while it was the softest landing I'd ever had, I ended up in surgery and physical therapy for many months.

When I went to get on him, nearly a year after my accident – I panicked, and couldn't. I was able to ride other horses... in a somewhat limited fashion... and after a 2-year hiatus from THAT horse, decided that enough was enough.

I set out to find an answer to my fears, to riding again, without panic, without anxiety, and I did indeed find answers.

You are NOT alone with your fear or anxiety about riding. While most equestrians don't speak of it, we ALL go through it. We ALL must face down that mental demon.

And as more and more equestrians are raising their hands, sharing their experiences with fear and with overcoming it, I know you (or the rider you care about) can too.

Happy Trails!

Intro

You may have absolute Self-Confidence in one area of your life (such as the career you trained for) and be totally unsure of yourself in another area(s). You probably know Self-Confidence when you see and experience it. It may be the advice from a trusted veterinarian or riding advice from a trusted trainer – if you don't feel that Self-Confidence, it's likely you won't take their advice.

Becoming the confident person you want to be may be especially difficult if you've lost self-esteem, or have experienced severe criticism in your life. As equestrians, we sometimes lose Self-Confidence due to an accident (on or off our horse), finding our riding skills are not well matched with our mount (over-horsed), or for other, sometimes unknown reasons.

 Even if you're well-trained in riding and handling horses, you may find it difficult to succeed if you lack Self-Confidence. For example, if you're a well-educated competitive rider, you may still find it hard to compete without feeling nervous and bumbling.

There are ways to overcome your lack of Self-Confidence and move on to the success which comes from the proper training, personal qualities and values and experience. No matter what areas of your life you need help in gathering Self-Confidence to succeed, you can do it with a little work and lots of patience.

How to Prepare Yourself for Self-Confidence

Preparing yourself to receive Self-Confidence boosters means that you first must understand what real Self-Confidence is. Some go overboard when pushing for more Self-Confidence and become aggressive, turning into drama queens. But, Self-Confidence is actually more self-efficacy and an innate sense of self-esteem rather than aggressiveness. Aggressiveness can too easily turn into bullying.

Self-Confidence is knowing that if you work hard, learn skills and meet goals, you'll reach the success you're striving for. Others need to sense your Self-Confidence – especially as equestrians, your HORSE needs to know you are confident – so you should learn to act and present yourself in a certain way which exudes it. People may assess Self-Confidence in you by the following ways:

1. **You take calculated risks**. When others know that you'll get the job done or may fearlessly set out on an unknown path, they'll have more Self-Confidence in your ability to lead.
2. **You don't need to brag about past achievements**. Others can be very put-off by bragging. Let your skills speak for themselves and others will begin to realize your achievements and admire you for them.
3. **You always do the right thing**. Even if it means going against the "crowd," you keep to your ethics and values.
4. **You are gracious**. Accept compliments gracefully rather than dismissing your accomplishments.
5. **You can admit your mistakes**. It takes a strong person to admit to mistakes, but others will think higher of you for the trait, especially if you turn the mistakes into learning experiences (a very important skill, as it turns out).

When you believe in yourself and your abilities, others will follow suit. Preparing to become confident in all you do should include the above traits. As you make them part of your life, you'll become more confident and sure of whatever challenge that comes your way.

Beginning the Self-Confidence Journey

Building Self-Confidence is a journey – not a quick fix. It's a process of first knowing yourself – especially your strengths and weaknesses and then taking steps to build on the strengths and downplay (or work on) the weaknesses. Begin the Self-Confidence journey with focus and determination and you'll rise to the Self-Confidence level you need to achieve true success.

Becoming a confident individual is very achievable. And, as you raise your Self-Confidence level, you'll also achieve success because of meeting and succeeding at challenges. Here are some steps you'll need to take to chart your Self-Confidence journey so you reach the finish line successfully:

- **Assess your life's accomplishments**. Don't limit yourself to work-related accomplishments. Are you a good parent – inspiring Self-Confidence in children and leading them by being a good example? Focus on these accomplishments and enjoy the success you've already achieved. Keeping a success journal is a very good way to do this.

- **Assess your strengths**. By looking at your accomplishments, you're likely going to see a pattern which reflects your true strengths. Your friends and family might cast light on your strengths and weaknesses, so be sure to seek advice from others to get the true picture. Again, journaling is a good way to do this.

- **Assess what you really want out of life**. You'll never be truly successful unless you're working toward a life goal. Making and achieving goals is key to gathering Self-Confidence you need to ultimately succeed. Again, journaling is a good way to do this.

- **Develop a positive mindset**. Defeating negative self-talk is one of the best things you can do to gain Self-Confidence. Negative self-talk is a Self-Confidence "killer," so you must learn how to replace the negative with positive thoughts and affirmations. Again, journaling is a good way to do this.

- **Commit to Self-Confidence**. When you commit to becoming more confident, you're also committing to success. The commitment should be a vow to yourself that you're in this for the long-run. When doubts begin to peek through, analyze them mindfully and discard the ones without merit while finding a way to overcome genuine risks. Again, journaling is a good way to do this.

If you lack Self-Confidence, you'll likely find it difficult to take risks and accept challenges. Too much Self-Confidence may render you arrogant and uninformed. Reaching a Self-Confidence balance is necessary to truly succeed.

Staying on Track

After determining your Self-Confidence level and get to know yourself better, you're ready to set goals that will keep you on track to reach the level of success you desire. You've got to know yourself – your strengths and weaknesses – so you'll know where to begin and how to get to the finish line of success.

That means that you don't begin by starting on the "high dive" of the pool. You'll begin slowly and achieve small accomplishments before you're ready to plunge in to the deep water.

As you might expect, the first goal to success should be gathering the knowledge you need to get to the top. Whether you're studying to be a physician or a seamstress, you've got to begin by identifying skills you're going to need in your chosen path. How do you get to where you want to be? It may involve school or personal training and it could take months or years, but it's a necessary step to achieving your long-term goals.

Begin with small goals. In the beginning, don't make the goals so difficult that you have trouble reaching them. Give yourself some slack and set some small, readily achievable goals and leave the more intense goals for later in the journey.

Accept that you're going to make mistakes and learn from them. Any time you're on an unfamiliar path, failure is bound to happen. Keep looking at your accomplishments and keep the positive thinking strong.

Keep Moving Toward the Ultimate Goal

Nothing gives you a sense of Self-Confidence like the act of moving toward your goal by celebrating the small achievements and reaching a big goal that you've set for yourself.

It's normal for Self-Confidence to waver at times. Frustration and doubts can set in and you may think you'll never be good enough to "get there." But, Self-Confidence can get you to your ultimate goal and help you push yourself harder until you finally achieve success.

Goal setting is the most important step to gaining the knowledge and experience you'll need to gain Self-Confidence. As you gain inner Self-Confidence, you'll begin to project that confident air to others.

It's not enough to talk about your goals or even to write them down. You've got to take serious action in taking part in and meeting the steps needed to turn those goals into realities. But, it's important to be effective in your goal-setting rather than simply mapping them out.

Here's how to set goals that are meaningful and which will increase your Self-Confidence level as you experience success of meeting them all:

- **Be specific**. Set goals which are precise – not arbitrary goals that aren't that important to the final outcome.
- **Assessing your success**. You'll need to figure out how you'll recognize your success. For example, if you're concentrating on losing weight, you can use the scales or measuring tape.
- **Set realistic goals.** Unless you're setting realistic and achievable goals, you won't be able to reach them and will end up frustrated and with even less Self-Confidence than you began with.
- **Set a time frame**. Always set goals with a time limit. Be realistic about how long it will take you to reach them. You may even need to change the long-term goal time, but you should have a good idea about when you should successfully reach the goal.
- **Set challenging goals**. You should be excited about the goal you're going after and challenged by the nature of it.

A systematic approach to goal-setting will increase your chances of achieving success. Along the way, stop awhile and assess your progress. Effective feedback can provide the information you need to keep on track and lessen your chances of giving up.

Also, review your goals periodically to be sure they're appropriate to your changing Self-Confidence level. Boosting Self-Confidence to set and reach goals is a technique used by most successful people today. Each challenge or idea can produce doubts and cause changes that can either knock you off the track to success – or keep you successfully in the success lane.

Reading List For Equestrians Working On Self-Confidence

Reading is a wonderful way to reprogram our minds. Here is a short list of books I recommend, as well as an ongoing list that I add to from time to time on Amazon.

- "**The New Pscho-Cybernetics**: The Original Science Of Self-Improvement And Success That Has Changed The Lives Of 30 Million People" – Maxwell Maltx
- "**Riding Fear Free**: Help For Fearful Riders And Their Teachers" – Laura Daley & Jennifer Becton
- "**Inside Your Ride**: Mental Skills For Being Happy and Successful with Your Horse" – Tonya Johnston
- "**Pressure Proof Your Riding**: Mental Training Techniques: Gain Self-Confidence and Get Motivated So

You (And Your Horse) Achieve Peak Performance" – Daniel Stewart

- **"Ride Right**: Balance Your Frame and Frame of Mind with an Unmounted Workout and Sports Psychology System" – Daniel Stewart
- **"Confident Rider, Confident Horse**: Build Your Self-Confidence And Develop A True Partnership With Your Horse From The Ground To The Saddle" – Anne Gage
- As well as an ongoing list located on Amazon... Visit http://RiderConfidenceTelesummit.com/bookz for the current book list.

Resource List For Equestrians Working On Self-Confidence

There are also a number of online courses designed specifically for riders with self-confidence issues – and more specifically, riding-specific confidence issues.

There are more than are listed here, but these are ones that I'm aware of.

- "De-Spook U" – http://De-SpookYou.com
- "Confident Riding Success" - www.confidentridingsuccess.com/
- Back In The Saddle Rider Recovery - http://backinthesaddleriderrecovery.com/

I'd love to know what you think about this little book, if it helps you in any way, and if you have any resources you'd like added to the list.

Happy Trails!

Patricia

Patricia Reszetylo

www.ingramcontent.com/pod-product-compliance
Lightning Source LLC
Chambersburg PA
CBHW062034280526
45787CB00005B/2316